# The Best of Kindness

## Origami Poems Project
## Kindness Contest 2016
## Winning & Select Poems

♦

### Editors
### Jan Keough & Kevin Keough

Copyright © 2016 by Origami Poems Project

All rights reserved. This book may not be reproduced or transmitted in any form or by any means, electronic or mechanical, including photocopying, recording, or by any information storage and retrieval systems, without permission in writing from the publisher.
Please contact us: origamipoems@gmail.com

Individual Poets retain all rights to their poems.

Published by:
Origami Poems Project
1948 Shore View Drive
Indialantic, FL 32903
www.origamipoems.com

Published April 2016

Cover image by Lauri Burke

The Best of Kindness:
Origami Poems Kindness Contest 2016
Winning and Select Poems
First Edition


Copyright © 2016 Origami Poems Project
All rights reserved.
ISBN-13: 978-0692671986 (Origami Poems Project)

ISBN-10: 0692671986

First Edition

# DEDICATION

To all who hope and work for a kinder world,
and to the poets whose words encourage us to keep trying,
this collection is dedicated.

...and in memory of our mini-schnauzer, Pixie, who
passed away on a quiet Sunday afternoon during the
creation of this anthology.

## Acknowledgments or in Gratitude

To Our Contest's Finalist Judge,
Peg Quinn
Poet, Artist, Overall Fair-minded Person
*

To Editor and Web Advisor,
Kevin Keough
Musician, Poet, Balanced Being
*

To Our Cover Artist Extraordinaire,
Lauri Burke
For her Creative Whimsy and Sense of Humor
*

To poet friends, near and far, for your steadfast encouragement,
we are thankful...
- *Jan Keough, Editor*

# The Best of Kindness
## An Anthology of Poems

Origami Poems Project
Kindness Contest 2016
Winning & Select Poems

Finalist Judge, Peg Quinn

Editors:
Jan Keough
Kevin Keough

## Introduction

We hadn't planned to publish an anthology when our contest opened. But it soon became clear to us that many of the poems should have a wider audience.

What did these poems tell us about *kindness*?

Well, we learned what kindness can be and what it is not. Often, it's neither grandiose nor noteworthy in a public sense (*Kindness* by M.j. Iuppa). Kindness has a quiet quality, of being hidden from view (*Saint of the Day*). Many poems serve as witness to a 'saving' moment (*The Untouchable*). Or show how this ineffable quality challenges (*Arms Wide Open*). Others ponder the significance of kindness (Is it *Natural* to be *Kind, Duplexity*) or see it from the plight of our muted brethren as in *Holstein.*

And kindness, it seems, can surprise the recipient (*Camellias*). In an instance, one heart crosses over to another (*Faith in Us*). And this response arises despite the overabundance of anger and violence hiding in memory (*Angel of Kindness*).

We see kindness flow with invisible tendrils to others (*The Difference Kindness Makes*) or manifest in deliberate efforts to teach (*Shut-Ins*). A stranger's glance (*Content*), seeing someone lost (*Kindness* by Bergquist ), receiving unexpected forgiveness (*Taking It Back*), or reflecting on our life (*All I Have*) can bring us to a better place (*The Poem I Should Have Written, What Do You Say?*).

That kindness appears without hesitation from creatures (*Left You In The Dark*) illuminates our actions.  On the other side of the spectrum, a painting in a gallery can challenge our hesitations (*Lesson*).  Kindness will manifest in the most simple of gestures (*Morning Gift*); creating an elegant balance of appreciation and love (*When She Cried*).

Lastly, life metes out conditions that defy understanding (*New Childhood*), try to overwhelm (*Ode to an Eleven Year Old Boy, Bedtime*) and test the boundaries of despair (*The Possum*). Our innermost selves reach out from these dark places (*What If*) and call for response (*Make Offerings, What do you say?*).  Yes, even a breeze or a reflective moment (*February*), introspective and perhaps fleeting, can uplift (*The River, Rosewood & Inlays*) with exuberance (*Years Later, Her Act of Loving Kindness*).

This anthology offers what moved us most.  It harbors only 41 poems from the 135 received.  We were very fortunate when Peg Quinn wholeheartedly agreed to be the finalist judge. Here is her all-too-modest bio:

'Peg Quinn's poetry has been published in numerous journals and anthologies and twice nominated for the Pushcart Prize.  She paints murals and theatrical sets and teaches art at a private school in Santa Barbara, California.'

Perhaps Peg's intrinsic qualities are best expressed by this quote she shared from a Wendell Berry poem:
    "Be joyful, though you have considered all the facts."

This says much about kindness, doesn't it?

*- Jan Keough*

NOTE:

This anthology presents poems in fluid categories of four to eight poems each. The category headings encourage a wide interpretation. Many of the poems could live quite comfortably within any of the sections.

These groupings are not meant to define or inhibit. Enjoy them as you would a tree-top canopy, filtering sunlight and shadow along the way.

Let's close with a quote by poet and essayist Gretel Ehrlich,

> "I realized happiness was a by-product of curiosity and surrender, not of pursuit and entitlement."

With abundant optimism, curiosity, and joy, we offer:

THE BEST OF KINDNESS

## The 2016 Origami Poems Kindness Contest

## Winning Poems

### First Place
**'Angel of Kindness'**
Cynthia Anderson

### Second Place
**'Faith In Us'**
Jeffrey Johannes

### Third Place
**'The Difference Kindness Makes'**
Jackie Chou

### Honorable Mention
**'Content'**
Marilyn Zelke-Windau
&
**'Saint of the Day'**
Jan Chronister

### Editor's Appreciation
**'Holstein'**
Gretchen Primack

# Contents

## LEARNING KINDNESS ................................................ 1

Faith in Us ............................................................. 3
Shut-Ins ................................................................ 4
Duplexity .............................................................. 5
Taking It Back ...................................................... 6
All I Have ............................................................. 8
Camellias ............................................................ 10
The River ........................................................... 12
Every Moment Passes and Every Moment Stays Still .. 13

## APPRECIATION ................................................ 15

The Difference Kindness Makes ........................ 17
Lesson ................................................................ 18
Content .............................................................. 20
Kindness ............................................................ 21
February ............................................................ 22
Dogs and Cats and Places ................................. 23
Errand ................................................................ 24

## INTROSPECTION ............................................. 27

Left You in the Dark ........................................ 29
Arms Wide Open .............................................. 30
Rosewood & Inlays ........................................... 32
Years Later ........................................................ 33

| | |
|---|---|
| The Poem I Should Have Written | 34 |
| The Ice | 35 |
| Two Kinds | 36 |
| Hearts | 38 |

## DILEMMA ............................................................41

| | |
|---|---|
| What If | 43 |
| Bedtime | 44 |
| Is It *Natural* to Be *Kind*, | 45 |
| Language Like Medicine | 46 |
| Morning Gift | 47 |

## IN PRAISE OF KINDNESS .................................49

| | |
|---|---|
| When She Cried | 51 |
| The Untouchable | 52 |
| Saint of the Day | 53 |
| Her Act of Loving Kindness | 54 |
| Kindness— | 55 |
| Make Offerings | 56 |
| Whatchamacallit | 58 |

## CHALLENGE .......................................................61

| | |
|---|---|
| Ode to an Eleven Year Old Boy | 63 |
| Angel of Kindness | 64 |
| Holstein | 66 |
| New Childhood | 68 |
| The Possum | 69 |
| What Do You Say? | 70 |

| | |
|---|---|
| About the Poets | 73 |
| Photographs | 101 |
| Cover Art | 103 |
| About The Origami Poems Project | 105 |
| Addendum: Quotes on Kindness | 107 |
| Index of Poets | 109 |

# LEARNING KINDNESS
### Observe, learn, respond

**Faith In Us** - Jeffrey Johannes
              • Winner, *2nd place*
**Shut-Ins** - Caroline Johnson
**Duplexity** - Tammi Truax
**Taking it Back** - Bryanna Licciardi
**All I Have** - Carol Ayer
**Camellias** - Sandra Anfang
**The River** - Maryann Russo
**Every Moment Passes And Every Moment Stays Still**
                                  - Martin Willitts Jr.

# Faith in Us
Jeffrey Johannes

Sometimes I choose
a spot on a quiet page
and write down
something unusual
such as the story of
how everyone
on a street
in Chinatown
walked carefully
while a woman chased
hundreds of tiny turtles
after they got loose
from a tank
in her market stall.
Not one turtle
was harmed.
And this mercy
lifts my spirits,
reminds me that
acts of kindness
appear like moths
circling our porch lights
drawn to the light.

•

Winner, **Second Place**
Origami Poems Kindness Contest 2016

# Shut-Ins
### Caroline Johnson

It is snowing softly. Mother grips
the steering wheel with gloved hands,
intent on our mission. She turns down

a tree-lined street and slowly pulls
up to a darkly-lit house with peeling
gray paint, sagging porch, so different

from the other Victorian houses with
perfect trim and lighted driveways.
I can smell the pine from the back

of our Buick, where a dozen wreaths
fill the seats, each tied with a homemade
red ribbon. "Here," she says, thrusting

a large one into my small hands.
"Go up there and ring the doorbell."
Numb, I blink and feel I am at the dentist

after the pricking of Novocain and a dull
toothache. "Go on," she says, pushing me
out the door. So I walk, my legs weak,

frozen, clutching the wreath tightly,
into the dark night and towards Mrs. Smith,
my first lesson in kindness.

# Duplexity
### Tammi Truax

See my grandparents, so long gone.
Their simple outfits; he in his undershirt
and green work khakis as always.

She in another version of her apron
and soft cotton blouse, just like the one
she put on me when I was sunburnt.

Both posing, hands at hips, resting
just a moment from some earthly
task they would soon return to.

And smiling; not big grins, but just
happy half-smiles, indulging a kid
they actually liked having around.

And the old duplex outhouse
by the stone wall, in the shadows
of a stand of trees behind them.

Two people who showed me
what love looks like, and
that we are meant to go through life

two by two.

# Taking It Back
### Bryanna Licciardi

> *...what he wanted seemed to have too many corners*
> *to come out of his mouth.*    —Stephen King

We're dancing the Tootsie Roll on my front lawn
when they spot Arlie riding her bike
with the training wheels. The girls laugh at her,
call her names, but she rides by without looking,
as if she doesn't need to know who we are.
Arli was my best friend until the older girls
started inviting me around. Normally I can look away
but today one of the girls hands me a willow branch,
says in a low voice, *Whip that nerd.*
Arlie's coming by again, and now I'm mad
she doesn't care what they think. And I'm jealous
she doesn't try hard, like me.
With the branch I run after her, swinging,
trying to ignore the way she cries out,
or the sharp sound it makes against her skin.
I want to take it back even as I'm doing it,
but she's gone off. After that, her mom keeps
Arlie away from me. Every few days
I stop by the house, only to be sent away.
I'm scared of what I did, but don't get why,
or don't want to, so I keep knocking,
and ignore the older girls who've started
laughing at me, too, until finally, weeks later,
Arlie answers next to her mom and lets me in.
We spend the afternoon in her backyard
sketching butterflies that eat from her feeder.

They never stay still enough for me,
but Arlie can draw them from memory.
I watch her tiny, pale fingers expertly
pull the pencil around the page
and I open my mouth to say something
but she looks up at me and smiles.
I don't know how she did it
but I don't want her to take it back
so I smile too. When they all fly away,
Arli invites me to their garden, showing me
how to catch roly polies, tells me to watch,
to let them curl up in our hands.

## All I Have
    Carol Ayer

Ludicrous, really, to compare one life to another,
especially mine
with its outrageous good fortune.

I ponder over which of a million products to buy;
I choose the ones that will help me lose weight.
Would a starving citizen of Somalia
grasp the meaning of a non-fat, sugar-free latte?

I strive for my comforter to match my sheets,
my sheets to match my blankets.
Would the homeless shivering along my route
appreciate that my bedding does not clash?

Would an Afghan mother mourning her dead son
ensure that her mascara, like mine,
is smearproof and waterproof?

My life, filled with its trivialities and unnecessary luxuries,
shames me.

And aware of the inadequacy
of my pennies, my prayers, and my good wishes,
I go to the market and smile at everyone I pass,
let a woman go ahead of me in line,
and banter with the cashier.

It does not feed the hungry.
It does not bring back the dead.
And, therefore, it is probably nothing.
Yet, maybe, just maybe, for that brief second,
because it is all I have,
it is, actually, everything.

●


Finalist
 - Origami Poems Kindness Contest 2016

# CAMELLIAS
### Sandra Anfang

In line at the posh market
I hug a homely cabbage to my chest
Put that on my tab,
the man before me gestures.
Such a token act
yet huge in spontaneity
rich in kindness.

At December's reading
a poet brings a Christmas Cactus
decked out in cerise.
In my haste to leave
"the red-eyed staff shooing us out"
I leave it on a table.

Maria takes it home
as I would have
not content to leave it orphaned.
I call the next day,
learn she's rescued it,
plans to return it on her evening shift.

I want to give it to her
"she of the soft eyes and tender voice"
but it's a special gift
so I choose a clutch of purple camellias
hand them up over the mahogany bar
like a child's gift of wildflowers.

You order coffee and a glass of wine.
When you return, you explain,
She wouldn't let me pay for this;
you're the first to ever give her flowers.

I take this in, feel a pain
like a flash of lightning bisect my heart.
I'll bring her flowers every month, I think.
I tuck this thought behind my ear
where good intentions roost.

# The River
### Maryann Russo

I wait for the river
to wash over me
to carry me
through its descending rapids

but I am afraid

of the rocks
jutting out of its folds
and the sharp edges
of fallen branches

My feet feel
the grit of the shallows
and  I wonder
what else lies there
to cut or to sting

I want the river
to carry me with kindness
around the bends
and trees that bow
from the banks

carry me safely
all the way
to the sea

# Every Moment Passes and Every Moment Stays Still
*A villanelle*
Martin Willitts Jr.


When I look down the browning grass hill
to December stilling the lake with thin ice
and the far off tree line is blue from the chill

further still I see the low lying flat thrill
of grey blue clouds making snow and blight
when I look down the browning grass hill

above is the break of light with absence and skill
of kindness from God making me feel nice
as a far off tree line is blue from the chill

and then in stillness I am no longer ill
as geese push away through day and night
when I look down the browning grass hill

how many days have we left and still
the lake has been here as chill continues to bite
and the far off tree line is blue from the chill

and from kindness to kindness nothing fails
this silence as geese take off in solemn flight
when I look down the browning grass hill
and the far off tree line is blue from the chill

# APPRECIATION
    Kindness may appear without warning

**The Difference Kindness Makes** – Jackie Chou •
                                   Winner, *3rd Place*
**Lesson** – James Penha
**Content** – Marilyn Zelke-Windau • *Honorable Mention*
**Kindness** – Peter Bergquist
**February** – Marguerite Keil Flanders
**Dogs and Cats and Places** – Frank Beltrano
**Errand** – Joely Johnson Mork

## The Difference Kindness Makes
Jackie Chou

If my father was alive
I would take you to meet him
in our humble abode in El Monte
He'd be sitting in a sofa
a stack of newspapers on his lap
He'd be looking up behind
thick myopic lenses
his eyes wide and good humored
He would nod his head and smile at you
Not scowl at you like my sister does

If my father was alive
you and I might be cruising down
the highway with the windows down
the soft afternoon breeze
would brush against our faces
as we head to a Chinese buffet restaurant
where we can eat fish fillet and sushi

If my father was alive
I may not have a nice car
or more money for clothes
but I might be slightly happier
for he would nod his head and smile at you
Instead of scowling at you like my sister does

•

Winner, **Third Place**
Origami Poems Kindness Contest 2016

# LESSON
    James Penha

*After Saint Francis (1600) by Federico Barocci*
*at the Metropolitan Museum of Art*

We are drawn by the light and drawn
to the center of the canvas
where the nail's head
with depth protrudes
from Francis' left hand—
stigmata arisen from within his palm
where it had always resided
waiting—
we wonder—
rather than hammered
with winds without?

But Francis does not wonder
or flinch
or even look
at one mere miracle.

His sanguine gaze
in oil light a lumen less
across
the canopy
of the grotto,
is on selflessness
(in shadow against
the afternoon storm)
still the source
of illumination
and perspective.

We who think
we see no kindness in the world
dare not follow Francis' eyes.
•


Finalist
- Origami Poems Kindness Contest 2016

# CONTENT
### Marilyn Zelke-Windau

Outside a restaurant in Chivay, Peru
the short-haired yellow dog
gazes furtively up at you
and away,
brings her head and brown eyes
down shyly, yet hopefully.

*Hola, perro*, you say.
Orbs raise, blink.
Tail wags, thumping the stucco wall
where you lean.
*Oh, you're a good dog.*
*You're such a good dog.* ☐

She sits, raises her paw,
presses your leg with kindness in return.

Confirming friendship,
she lays down, rests her chin
on your shoe,
content to be near you and rest.
•

Honorable Mention
Origami Poems Kindness Contest 2016

# KINDNESS
    Peter Bergquist

Looking out a hotel window,
I see some stranger
help a blind man cross the street
and think of my mother
on a night when I was young:

>Our family drove downtown
>to the premiere of a movie,
>Hitchcock's North By Northwest.
>We stood waiting in a line
>wrapped around the block.
>
>Down the sidewalk came
>a grubby, stubbled little man,
>tapping with his red-tipped cane,
>baffled by the unfamiliar noise and bump,
>frozen finally in his fear.
>
>Mom moved to help,
>took him gently by the arm,
>told him what was happening
>and led him to his bus stop at the corner.

She alone, of all the people there, did this.
What better could be said of anyone?

# February
### Marguerite Keil Flanders

Sun slants through
the shutters
of bare branches.
Jays flash in
blue sky. Cold
does me a favor,
clears away
dichotomies,
makes room
for unity.
I stand
on one foot,
or hang
upside down.
I am free,
awake to all
and asleep
at the same time.
Opposites
marry. I stand
in infinite kindness
under an oak.
Jays scold me;
I smile and
love them back.

## Dogs and Cats and Places
    Frank Beltrano

*After page 18 of Xu Bing's novel "Book From the Ground" written entirely in pictograms*

Would you like my dog?
In my new apartment
I can't have a dog.

I would love your dog
but in my house
I already have a cat.

I really love my cat
so I can't provide a home
for your adorable dog.

I feel like a dog
that I can't provide a place
but when I got my cat

Rebecca wanted a dog.
Maybe she has room
in her heart for your dog.

# Errand
### Joely Johnson Mork

Once in a while
I leave my apartment
and go to Nick's Grocery
where the man behind the counter is
of Middle-Eastern descent.

I like the special way
he proudly displays the
two kinds of ZigZag cigarette paper
offered for sale.

On my way home
I take a left on Octavia,
and the prostitutes are already
congregating on the corner.

When I pass I always nod.
When she asks me for a cigarette
I stand, bags in hand,
and let her roll her own.

# INTROSPECTION
    Time, effort, awareness…

**Left You In the Dark** – Chris Toto Zaremba
**Arms Wide Open** – Bill Carpenter
**Rosewood & Inlays** – silent lotus
**Years Later** – Mary McCarthy
**The Poem I Should Have Written** – Charlene Neely
**The Ice** – Padma Prasad
**Two Kinds** – D.G. Geis
**Hearts** – Joan Leotta

## Left You in the Dark
### Chris Toto Zaremba

I am sorry I left you in the dark again.
I was wrapped up in my world and lost track of time.
Daylight turned to night and you wondered
how long it had been, and if I would come back,
and if you did something wrong.
No one lit the porch light for me to find my way.
I was sure you would be upset, sitting there waiting.
But your eyes lit up when I opened the door.
You were so kind to bring me your favorite toy.
Your tail wagged so hard that I knew you still loved me.
I am so sorry I left you in the dark again.
•

Finalist
– Origami Poems Kindness Contest 2016

# Arms Wide Open
### Bill Carpenter

Kindness seems
a cast-off suit of clothes,
more fitting centuries past.

Many suspect it's a guise
to win favor,
or more nefarious purpose.

A friend once observed
I was not
"much used to kind treatment,"

although given more than most-
a loving mother, a father who spent
his much-abused generosity on neighbors

but little or none at home,
perhaps explaining why
it seemed to me a fool's cloak,

or viewed analytically
an agent for the ego's designs
the libido's desires.

I often resolve to restore
its sweetness to my life,
stumbling along its path,

asking myself
what I hope to gain
with such a posture

arms wide open
like some long-suffering savior
marching to Calvary.
•

Finalist
 - Origami Poems Kindness Contest 2016

## Rosewood & Inlays
    silent lotus

*unaccomplished troubadours like mocking birds at the edge of waterfalls .*
. .replayed over and over in my head as if nothing else mattered as if all i had heard before was nothing more than latent tumbleweed

i left little white tickets with hand written prices on sophisticated undergarments and went out to the café across the street i needed to become the tenderness of anonymous

i return every year to remind myself of my self   and why it was that my mother met my father here    why    i sat down across            from

 you

# Years Later
### Mary McCarthy

And still you bring me
gifts unlooked for
generous, surprising
beyond anything
I could have earned.
Each day you unroll
hours full of joy,
turning and changing
like a skyful of wind,
like water moving
over rocks, like your
expressions, always
different, always
the same. Without you
the days are flat,
the wind dies,
the water freezes up,
the sky is empty,
and I am lost, an orphan
out of time, homeless
and alone, without even
a box to call my own.
•

Finalist
– Origami Poems Kindness Contest 2016

# The Poem I Should Have Written
## Charlene Neely

The poet at the next table
has borrowed paper and a pen.
Unexpected and unprepared,
her muse has struck.
While I have struggled
with these few lines,
she has filled a whole page
and is turning it sidewise
to obliterate the margins.
Did I give her the one
magic sheet of paper
in the whole notebook
with words invisibly imbedded
just waiting for someone
to pronounce the proper incantation
allowing them to appear.

# THE ICE
### Padma Prasad

The black birds crack sunflower seeds;
The yellow birds feed on reddish pips.
In the bird food packet, there's many kinds,
I suppose for each particular beak.

I must be particular to keep
The bird feeder always full -
Hunger rewrites the scriptures
Thirst will bestow dark.

This winter, kindness formed
In my head, like the ice upon the pond;
The birds walked across on it,
To where it was spring.

## Two Kinds
### D.G. Geis

We delight
when animals act like people

but are appalled
when people act like people.

A kitten on a skateboard
frames sentiment perfectly,

but a fat woman in the buffet line
merits only contempt.

Perhaps kindness has more to do
with being one kind of person.

The kind of person
who is the same person all the time

and kindly views all people
as being of one kind.

Because to pay in kind
is not always kind,

and though we are taught not to confuse
the noun with the adjective,

perhaps it would be better
to throw caution to the wind

so that the noun which means
"Fundamental nature or quality"

is combined with the adjective
meaning "compassionate, considerate and loving."

The two kinds would then be one
and the resulting word would mean,

quite unambiguously,
 a kind that is

more of the same

# HEARTS
### Joan Leotta

Hearts power
engines of transubstantiation
feelings become ideas
ideas become words.
Words become deeds:
deeds build lives—
testaments of love or
monuments to pain.
Depending on
what's in the heart.


Note:  An earlier version of *Hearts* was posted February 2016 on Tupelo Press 30/30

# DILEMMA
Choices made

**What If** – Elizabeth S. Wolfe
**Bedtime** – Helen D'Ordine
**Is It** *Natural* **To Be** *Kind* – George Such
**Language Like Medicine** – Ann Kestner
**Morning Gift** – Mary C. Rowin

# WHAT IF
    Elizabeth S. Wolf

What if today
there were no shootings.
What if today, there were no
beatings, even if dinner is
late or cold. What if today
everyone had enough dinner.
What if today, those who call themselves
lovers actually respected each other.
What if today, children were
seen and believed and
treasured. What if today
we greeted our neighbors.
What if today
is all the time we have;
what if today
is enough;
what if.

"What If"© Elizabeth S. Wolf, appeared in *Scarlet Leaf Review*, Issue 3, March 15 2016. Used with permission. www.scarletleafreview.com

## Bedtime
    Helen M. D'Ordine

He smiles, remembering when passion
raged between them.
They stand embracing;
two bodies pressed together.

Holding on, their faces and lips touch.
He calls her *Peaches*
a nickname from bygone days.
Sometimes she responds.

In sickness and in health, everything and
nothing have changed.
She lives among the broken bodies and shut-in minds.
He, the faithful visitor
loving
'til death do them part.

## Is It *Natural* to Be *Kind,*
    George Such

as the word's origin suggests, like
drinking water when filled with thirst
or sleeping when we are tired, an inborn
quality that helps kinfolk survive, an instinct
that greases community existence, or does it come
from the teaching of the tribe and our painful experience,
of seeing our posture as crooked, and wanting to stand straight?

## Language Like Medicine
Ann Kestner

Nothing I said intended
        your anger or
        meant to trigger
        bad memory.
        Maybe only hoped
        to change the story.

I was speaking in prayers
        not curses, my words
        wanting to be blessings
        wishing a soft spoken
        sentence could forgive
        you from your history.

I was only talking
        a language like medicine
        not expecting bad reaction.

Still I will tell you
        I love you
        again and again.

## Morning Gift
    Mary C. Rowin

Each morning I rise,
put away dishes;
I open the blinds,
brew some fresh coffee.

I try to create
order from chaos;
bring light to the dark,
nurture the morning.

Gifts for my husband?
I do it for me.
For him, it's simply
collateral benevolence.

# IN PRAISE OF KINDNESS
### Greatest to least and in-between

**When She Cried** – Christina Sng
**The Untouchable** – Susan Furst
**Saint of the Day** – Jan Chronister • *Honorable Mention*
**Her Act of Loving Kindness** – Roz Levine
**Kindness** – M.j. Iuppa
**Make Offerings** – Carol Aronoff
**Whatchamacallit** – Shittu Fowara

## WHEN SHE CRIED
    Christina Sng

You held her when she cried,
Soothing her with a song
Till I picked her up,
Grateful she had you to hold.
•

Finalist
– Origami Poems Kindness Contest 2016

# THE UNTOUCHABLE
## Susan Beth Furst

A filthy pink dress
barefoot and hungry
she looks away
invisible -
An old woman
reaches down
touches her face
and kisses her cheek
all she has to give -
The child looks up
and smiles

# SAINT OF THE DAY
### Jan Chronister

In class she knits prayer shawls.
Smooth yarn rolls between her fingers
like rosary beads. Each stitch
a wish for recovery from sickness
heartache, addiction. By noon

she is halfway there. The instructor
frowns at her, blind to the work
of her soul.
•

Honorable Mention
Origami Poems Kindness Contest 2016

# Her Act of Loving Kindness
Roz Levine

Our support group of people with serious illnesses
Was with Charlie as his strong man body disappeared
And ALS took control of his arms, legs and functions.
We helped to shore him up on his weekly climb
Of twenty steps to reach the meeting room in LA.

The strong among us were there to lift his wheelchair
When his legs no longer worked. We helped feed him
When his arms and hands withered to almost useless
Appendages. Our group held on to every whispered croak
As his voice grew to almost inaudible sounds. Charlie said
He was ready for his life to be over but had one final wish.
Pam, with her two missing breasts stepped up to the plate
She said, *I'm in*. The two of them spent one weekend together
Where she lavished him with kisses and loving kindness.

# Kindness—
    M.j. Iuppa

hardly a coincidence, fresh
loaf of bread on the cutting
board, waiting to be sliced, toasted
& served with butter & fig jam, with-
out a second thought.
•

Finalist
– Origami Poems Kindness Contest 2016

## Make Offerings
### Carol Aronoff

to those you venerate:
Buddha, Bodhisattvas, the ones
who dedicate their lives for us.
Jesus, Mary, Mother of mercy, all the saints
who help us with everyday things.
Burn incense for the Unnamable Divine.
Offer prayers to Deities, to mythic gods
and goddesses. To One or Many,
to the All. Remember the Ancestors.

When you're out in Nature, build a shrine
of stones and flowers. A single piece of fruit
will do. Feel the rain of blessings, then offer them
to city dwellers, to those who live in caves.

When you're eating offer food to those have none
and pray that everyone can eat as well as you do.
Light a candle for those in darkness. Light the room
with gratitude for whatever you can think of.

Offer up everything: night terrors, the bliss of loving freely,
hopes and fears that make us human and bind us
to each other. Feed the hungry ghosts.

When you're down or lonely, make offerings.
When you're waiting for your ride and traffic jams
will make you late, make offerings. Use your imagination.

Always give more than you receive. A smile, a large gratuity
for the waitress working two shifts in a row.
Kiss the postman for not opening your mail.

Make a gift of oranges to the local pastor,
no matter his affiliation or beliefs.

Worship generosity; you cannot share too much.
If you give everything away, especially what's most precious,
you'll find that you have more than you ever dreamed of.
When you are ill, pray that through your illness
others will not suffer. Offer them your healing
and exchange it for their misery or pain.

Breathe in the hardship, breathe in the violence of the world.
Breathe out your love and let it radiate to fill all space.
Keep something in your pocket for those who have less.
Help clear your elderly neighbor's yard. Fertilize her lawn
with kindness. Kindness, the key.

Make every moment an offering. Supplicate for peace.
Sing the praises of garbage collectors and window cleaners.
Prostrate to waterfalls and elephants. Call on Tara,
St. Theresa, on travelers who've learned to help
in war-torn places.

Each prayer of thankfulness, each petition will set a butterfly
free and warm the hand of a political prisoner, giving small
comfort. Light butter lamps and bonfires. Dance hula for Pele.
Make offerings as if your life depended on it.

# WHATCHAMACALLIT
## Shittu Fowora

we are all potters and words
are the plasticines
with which we cast our stories

to be an artist, is to be kind
with words,
is to stretch the edges of histories
is to go beyond the known
is to paint mischief with gamble
through unlived burners, glaze it
adroitly and let it flare
with time in the furnace with fragrance

artistry is humility styled in grace, a random act
of compassion, a tender song sang
a brush stroke on canvas
let's say all is done that's human
and earthly and heavenly,
and all is stormed and rained and settled.

there comes a rainbow, bowed across the globe,
calling out your little niece or slighted sister –
spurring her to come see for herself:
this, we call art.

# CHALLENGE
Struggle, loss, resolution


**Ode to an Eleven Year Old Boy** – Ronnie Hess
**Angel of Kindness** – Cynthia Anderson
　　　　　　　　　　　• Winner, *1st Place*
**Holstein** – Gretchen Primack • *Editor's Appreciation*
**New Childhood** – Helen Burke
**The Possum** – Marybeth Rua-Larsen
**What do you say?** – David Allen Sullivan

## Ode to an Eleven Year Old Boy
Ronnie Hess

His parents said, Thank you
were his first words.
As if he knew everything
had been a gift.
As for the rest,
he was a perfect boy,
had led a perfect life.
But the world deals roughly
with gratitude, promise, inadvertence,
a bright morning like no other,
a car and a bicycle that veer too close.
Now, blue and white balloons
line the procession route to church,
the colors of the swimming team
to which the child belonged.
Now, neighbors walk the sorrow path,
imagining too-late solutions:
a bridge over the roadway, no median,
tighter speed controls.
He could have been our son.

## Angel of Kindness
Cynthia Anderson

It never rains in
Southern California—
but man, it pours.
I'm at the toy store
when a curtain of water
hits, laced with hail.
No other shoppers,
so the clerk and I go
under the awning
to watch. We laugh
and laugh, there's
nothing else to do.
Back inside, he leans
on the counter, says,
*It used to rain like this
in Vietnam—two or
three times a day.
You couldn't tell
which way the bullets
were coming from.*
We are quiet.
You never got dry,
then, I say. *No, and
it got so you didn't
care anymore.*
For a moment
he's far gone,
down a dark road—
but he comes to,

resuming his life
as an angel of kindness.
He hands a balloon
to a crying baby,
and finds a reversible
doll for my niece's
birthday—Peter Pan
and Captain Hook,
two sides of the coin
that was wagered
in his name.
•


Winner, **First Place**
Origami Poems Kindness Contest 2016

# HOLSTEIN
### Gretchen Primack

I was also a child.
And also had one,
and another a year after,
and another,
and could not touch

even one.
Had I been born into a kinder
world, my milk would have been
for them. No one would have pulled
my children from my body

to crates, their lungs
full of loss.
Had I lived in a kind world,
long stretches of me
would have weaved
in the stretches of the world,

my natural-born children
taking in the milk I created
for them, not for a trade
of strangers,
and my life would have been mine
and theirs

as long as my body wanted life.
Child, put your head where our kind
is never allowed: at my flank,
at the great spill of me. Smell me
from your bent neck.
•


  Editor's Appreciation
Origami Poems Kindness Contest 2016

# New Childhood
### Helen Burke

In this our new religion
You feed me, clothe me, bathe me
And when people come and ask how we are
We smile and say ..we are fine and dandy ..doing good.
And our hearts beat a little faster at the mask we wear.
A mask is not new to us
And we are adept at wearing.
Like a shell at the sea's edge ..i lean on you and you on me.
The birds of the air pull us through another day.
The song of the ocean is you
And I am a small sparrow
Diving into the midnight hours of morning.
Outside my window a blackbird asks how we are
And him we can tell.
You pour me a glass of wine
It is the colour of fine roses
And we drift and dream into the heart of it.
We sew each other back together
Watch *Rebel Without a Cause*
And thank our lucky lucky stars
That the moon has been ours to take as lover
…one more time.
•


Finalist
 - Origami Poems Kindness Contest 2016

# The Possum
### Marybeth Rua-Larsen

That spring distracted us with rain. We dashed
from playpens full of ducklings to owl coops,
confirmed no birds were drowning and our rash
of hatchlings fed. Inside, we tended groups

of babies: squirrels, rabbits, ground hogs -- all
in need of formula. At dusk, a burst
of wind then her, drenched, with a possum sprawled
in her arms, dead, and newborns trying to nurse.

She found them on the white line, the fog
so thick they'd blended into mist. She zipped
them in her coat, raced them here, and shrugged,
expecting us to fix this: You're equipped.

Too young. Too cold. Too wet - they wouldn't make it.
We wrapped them in a new baby's blanket.

# What Do You Say?
## David Allen Sullivan

Let me write us into the place
where we're not in this argument—
the days and hours and seasons
of it—the silences you hold onto,
then me, the way it shapes itself
beyond known content, no longer
about what it was about, becoming
clear only in the cartography of our
losses. Let me write of the place
beyond this place, when we'll
travel the same river in the same
boat. Sometimes, my love, I think
it's the last divide that divides us,
that sense of togetherness we know
we'll lose when one of the other of us
dies that tightens us, skips us out
of the present like an erratic heart.
I know we'll be there soon, pull
the canoe up onto a bank and break
bread on an outspread picnic cloth.
Then you or I will lay our head
on the other's stomach and laugh,
there, on the other shore of sorrow.
I will write us into that existence,
I will send this missive to you,
whom I, too often, miss.

# About the Poets

## About the Poets

**Ann Kestner** is founder and editor of *Poetry Breakfast*. For over 20 years, her work has appeared in various publications. She spent most of her life in Virginia at the edge of the D.C. suburbs and now lives in New Jersey along the Raritan Bay.


**Bill Carpenter** is a widely published poet and member of the Ocean State Poets, whose mission is to provide an environment for self-expression through poetry to prisoners, nursing home residents and students in schools for the developmentally disabled. His book of poetry, *Templates*, is for sale through Amazon. His poem 'Peace' recently received Honorable Mention in the Barbara Mandigo Kelly Peace Poetry Contest. He lives in Chepachet, RI with his partner, Emily. They believe retirement is an opportunity to reinvent oneself through education and the arts.


**Bryanna Licciardi** received her MFA in Poetry from Emerson College. Her work has appeared in such journals as *Poetry Quarterly, Dual Coast Magazine, 491 Magazine, Adirondack Review, Dos Passos,* and *Blazevox*. www.bryannalicciardi.com

**Carol Aronoff**'s poetry has appeared in numerous journals and anthologies: Comstock Review, Poetica, Mindprints, HeartLodge, Sendero, Iodine, Tiger's Eye, Asphodel, Bosque; Cradle Songs, Before There is Nowhere to Stand, Women Write Resistance, 200 New Mexico Poems, Malala. A Pushcart Prize nominee, her illustrated book, The Nature of Music was published in 2005, Cornsilk in 2006, Her Soup Made the Moon Weep in 2007, Blessings From an Unseen World in 2013 and Dreaming Earth's Body in 2015. Currently, she resides in rural Hawaii--working her land, meditating in nature and writing.


**Carol Ayer**'s poetry has been published by *Poetry Quarterly, flashquake, Poesia,* and *Every Day Poets.* Carol lives in Northern California.   www.carolayer.com.


**Caroline Johnson** has two poetry chapbooks, Where the Street Ends and My Mother's Artwork, and has published poetry in Lunch Ticket, Uproot, Chicago Tribune, The Quotable, Rambunctious Review, New Scriptor, Avocet, and others.  A Pushcart Prize nominee, she won 1st place in the Chicago Tribune's Printers Row 2012 Poetry Contest. She teaches community college English in the Chicago area and is working on a poetry manuscript about caregiving.  http://jupiter-caroline.blogspot.com

**Charlene Neely** is a firm believer of Random Acts of Kindness and Random Acts of Poetry, so how could one go wrong with the Origami Poems Project? She also randomly hands out poetry bookmarks at the drop of a hat. Her new book of poetry and photographs, *The Lights of Lincoln*, will be out soon.

**Christina Sng** is a poet, writer, and artist. She lives in Singapore with her family and their gray tabby cat. Visit her: www.christinasng.com

**Chris Toto Zaremba** loves to have fun with words. She lets them run free on the south shore of Boston at the Catbird Cafe, Plymouth Center for the Arts, Mt. Hope Coffee House and at any other willing or unwilling venue that will let her have her say. She is working on her first children's book, *Angel of the Harbor*.

**Cynthia Anderson** lives in the Mojave Desert near Joshua Tree National Park. Her poetry collections include *In the Mojave, Desert Dweller, Shared Visions I and II,* and *Mythic Rockscapes*. She frequently collaborates with her husband, photographer Bill Dahl. Cynthia co-edited the anthology, *A Bird Black As the Sun: California Poets on Crows & Ravens*.

**David Allen Sullivan**'s books include: *Strong-Armed Angels, Every Seed of the Pomegranate*, a book of translation from the Arabic of Iraqi Adnan Al-Sayegh, *Bombs Have Not Breakfasted Yet*, and *Black Ice*. Most recently, he won the Mary Ballard Chapbook poetry prize for *Take Wing*. He teaches at Cabrillo College, where he edits the *Porter Gulch Review* with his students, and lives in Santa Cruz with his family. http://davidallensullivan.weebly.com


**D.G. Geis** lives in Houston, Texas. He degrees from the University of Houston (BA English) and California State University (MA Philosophy). Having published extensively both here and abroad, he is editor-at-large of Tamsen. https://tamsenblog.wordpress.com


**Elizabeth S. Wolf** lives in Massachusetts with her daughter and several pets. By day she works as a Metadata Librarian. Elizabeth has published poems in anthologies (*Merrimac Mic: Gleanings from the First Year; Amherst Storybook Project; Mosaics: A Collection of Independent Women, Volume 1*). Elizabeth's poetry has appeared in the online journals *NewVerseNews* and *Scarlet Leaf Review*. Three poems are forthcoming in *Peregrine Journal*.

**Frank Beltrano,** active member of the dynamic poetry community of London, Ontario, Canada, he gives public readings regularly. On several occasions he has read one of his poems as a warm-up to the readings of visiting poets of national renown, and has introduced poets on behalf of Poetry London. He has been a judge for the Western University undergraduate poetry competition, and is a reader for TLR (The Literary Review). Frank encourages aspiring adults to become practicing writers by co-facilitating a creative writing workshop series called the Writers' Eye View; he finds time to write daily and often is published in literary journals and anthologies.


**George Such** is currently a third-year English Ph.D. student at University of Louisiana Lafayette, where he has been awarded a University Fellowship. In a previous incarnation he was a chiropractor for twenty-seven years in eastern Washington. His poetry has appeared in *Arroyo Literary Review, Barely South Review, The Cape Rock, Dislocate, The Evansville Review,* and many other literary journals, his nonfiction in *Phoebe*, and his collection of poems *Where the Body Lives* was selected as winner of the 2012 Tiger's Eye Chapbook Contest (Tiger's Eye Press).

**Gretchen Primack** is the author of two poetry collections, *Doris' Red Spaces* (Mayapple Press 2014) and *Kind* (Post-Traumatic Press 2013). Her poems have appeared in *The Paris Review, Prairie Schooner, Field, Poet Lore, Ploughshares*, and other journals. Also an animal advocate, she co-wrote the memoir *The Lucky Ones: My Passionate Fight for Farm Animals* (Penguin Avery 2012). www.gretchenprimack.com

**Helen Burke** has amassed an impressive record of competition victories including the Torbay Prize 2013, Manchester International, the Devon and Dorset, the Suffolk Poetry Prize, the Sheffield Poetstars, and the Ilkley Literature Performance Poetry Prize (twice). Her work has been published in *Rialto, New Welsh Review, Northwords, Oxford Magazine, Dreamcatcher,* and *The Origami Poems Project* as well as in numerous anthologies and pamphlets. Helen's recent poetry collections include *The Ruby Slippers*, 2011, *Here's Looking at You Kid*, 2014, and *Today the Birds will Sing: Collected Poems*, June 2016 - all published by Valley Press.

**Helen M. D'Ordine,** retired teacher, former adjunct professor at Rhode Island College, former member of The Writers' Circle, Block Island Poetry Project participant, RI Writing Project Fellow, Ocean State Poet and Origami Poet. In 2011, she published a chapbook, *Conclusive Illusions.* Her poems have appeared in *Mobius, RI Writers' Circle Anthology, The Providence Journal: Poetry Corner, sheShines, Medicine & Health/RI, Where Beach Meets Ocean* (10 years, Block Island Poetry Project Anthology), *the Wickford Art Association: Poetry and Art (2013-2015),* and other publications.

**Jackie Chou** has been writing poetry since high school, winning the Lincoln High School junior class poetry contest with her poem 'Vanity Gate,' and went on to study Creative Writing at the University of Southern California. After graduating in 1997, she continued to write. In 2012, Miss Chou joined the Emerging Urban Poets' Workshop at the Santa Catalina Branch Library in Pasadena. Her poetry has been published in the *San Gabriel Valley Poetry Quarterly, The Alta Dena Poetry Review, Spectrum, Dryland Literary Magazine, Angel City Review Literary Magazine,* and *The Muses Gallery.*


A native New Yorker, **James Penha** has lived for the past quarter-century in Indonesia. He has been nominated for Pushcart Prizes in fiction and in poetry. *Snakes and Angels*, a collection of his adaptations of classic Indonesian folk tales, won the 2009 Cervena Barva Press fiction chapbook contest; *No Bones to Carry*, a volume of his poetry, earned the 2007 New Sins Press Editors' Choice Award. Penha edits TheNewVerse.News, an online journal of current-events poetry. @JamesPenha


**Jan Chronister** recently retired from teaching writing at a tribal college in Minnesota. She lives in Maple, Wisconsin with her husband and a crabby cat.

**Jeffrey Johannes** is an artist and poet. He co-edited the 2012 Wisconsin Poets' Calendar with his wife, Joan. He is currently combining his art and poetry to create comics, which he calls "pometoons". He lives in Port Edwards, Wisconsin. Visit his website, Book That Poet, at http://bookthatpoet.com/

**Joan Leotta** has been playing with words on paper and stage since childhood. Author, Story Performer, she encourages words through Pen and Performance - *Giulia Goes to War, Letters from Korea, A Bowl of Rice, Secrets of the Heart* - Desert Breeze Publishing & Amazon, *Simply a Smile*--collection of Short Stories - Cane Hollow Press & Amazon, *WHOOSH!* Picture book from TheaQ & Amazon. www.joanleotta.wordpress.com

**Joely Johnson Mork** is a writer and editor. She lives in Seattle. Learn more about her at www.joelyjohnsonmork.com.

**Marguerite Keil Flanders** is one of the founding members of Ocean State Poets, a group whose mission is to bring poetry to communities all across Rhode Island. She has led workshops in libraries, schools, at conferences and for Women's Centers. For the last 7 years she has been part of a team that runs a poetry group in the Men's Medium Security prison in Cranston, RI. She loves poetry: reading it and writing it is her way of tasting life. Margie is the author of a poetry collection, *The Persuasive Beauty of Imperfection*.

**Marilyn Zelke-Windau** is a Wisconsin poet, a former elementary school art teacher, and a worldwide traveler. Her writings have appeared in many printed and online journals, as well as in several anthologies. Her chapbook, "Adventures in Paradise" (Finishing Line Press) and her self-illustrated full-length book "Momentary Ordinary" (Pebblebrook Press) were published in 2014. She includes her maiden name when she writes to honor her father, who was also a writer.

**Martin Willitts Jr.**, retired librarian, has won the 2014 Broadsided award; 2014 Dylan Thomas International Poetry Contest; and, Rattle Ekphrastic Challenge, June 2015, Editor's Choice. He has many Origami Poems booklets, over 20 chapbooks of poetry; plus 11 full-length collections including *Irises, the Lightning Conductor For Van Gogh's Illness* (Aldrich Press, 2014), *God Is Not Amused with What You Are Doing in Her Name* (Aldrich Press, 2015), *How to Be Silent* (FutureCycle Press, 2016).

**Maryann Russo**'s poems have appeared in numerous publications. Maryann's work invites readers to return to the place that has always been within, often using the natural world as a bridge. One of her poems was nominated for the prestigious Pushcart Prize. She is publishing her second book of poetry, *I Wait For the River*. Maryann is a psychotherapist who lives and works in Southern California. Visit her on Facebook at MaryannRussoAuthor.

**Marybeth Rua-Larsen** lives on the south coast of Massachusetts. A freelance writer for Salem Press, she teaches part-time at Bristol Community College. Her poems, essays, flash fiction and reviews have appeared or are forthcoming in *American Arts Quarterly, The Raintown Review, Cleaver, Measure, the Cape Cod Poetry Review*, and the anthology *The Doll Collection*, edited by Diane Lockward. She won the 2011 Over the Edge New Writer of the Year Competition in Poetry in Galway, Ireland, and her chapbook *Nothing In-Between* was published by Barefoot Muse Press.


**Mary C. Rowin**'s poems have been published by the Wisconsin Fellowship of Poetry, *Stoneboat, Solitary Plover, Mariposa, Zo Magazine, Blue Heron, Postcard Poems and Pros,e* and by the Science Fiction Poetry Association. Mary's work has appeared in several anthologies, including The Ariel Project, Anthology of Poetry and Art. Mary lives in Middleton, WI and blogs at poeticpossibilities.wordpress.com.


**Mary McCarthy** has always been a writer but spent most of her working life as a Registered Nurse. She has been a Pushcart nominee, and has had work published in many print and online journals, including *Earth's Daughters, Third Wednesday*, and *Gnarled Oak*. Despite the grim realities of the world as it is now, she holds great hope for the future.

**M.j. Iuppa** lives on a small farm near the shores of Lake Ontario. She is Director of the Visual and Performing Arts Minor at St. John Fisher College. Her third full length poetry collection *Small Worlds Floating* is forthcoming from Cherry Grove Collections, August, 2016.
mjiuppa.blogspot.com


**Padma Prasad** is writer, painter and graphic artist, whose work has appeared in *Eclectica, The Looseleaf Tea, Reading Hour, ETA,* and *The Boiler Journal.* She blogs poem drawings at padhma.wordpress.com. Her art, mostly figurative, can be seen at //fineartamerica.com/profiles/padma-prasad.html. In writing, she tries to capture stillness; in painting, she tries to paint narratives. She lives in Northern Virginia.


**Peter Bergquist** earned a BA in English from Princeton University and an MFA in Creative Writing from Antioch University LA. His poems have been published in *Rougarou, The Queen City Review, The New Verse News, A Handful of Dust* and *The Broad River Review* among others. His poems "Gristle on the Bone," "The Easy Winter" and "Pulled Over Outside Santa Fe" were finalists for the latter journal's Rash Awards. He has published two novels: *Where the West Ends* and *A Wild Surmise*. A third, *Destiny's End*, is forthcoming and will conclude his *Manifest Trilogy*.

**Ronnie Hess** is a journalist and poet whose work has appeared in national and regional newspapers, magazines and literary journals. She is the author of a culinary travel guide, *Eat Smart in France*; and three poetry chapbooks, *Whole Cloth, Ribbon of Sand,* and *A Woman in Vegetable*. She lives in Wisconsin. www.ronniehess.com


**Roz Levine**, a member of the Los Angeles Poets and Writers Collective. Her work has appeared in several venues including *Cultural Weekly, The Sun, Pulse, Blink/Ink* and *The Ghazal Page*. Roz's writing life has helped her overcome many serious illnesses and she is forever grateful to have lived long enough to be called Grandma.


**Sandra Anfang**, poet, teacher, visual artist, her poems have appeared in *Poetalk, San Francisco Peace and Hope, West Trestle Review, Tower Journal, Clementine, Unbroken, River Poets' Journal, Spillway* and others. She is a California Poet/Teacher in the Schools and hosts a monthly poetry series in Petaluma. A chapbook, *Looking Glass Heart*, is forthcoming from Finishing Line Press. For her, to write is to breathe.

Storyteller, poet, freelance writer, and editor. **Shittu Fowora**, a lifelong fan of history and the power of scented words has recently been motivated by the winsomeness of birds and the wisdom of ants. Having been stung more than twice while attempting to lounge in trees to write verses, he now spends more time around PCs and electronic gadgets, at other times, he's in bed, not sleeping. His works have recently appeared in or forthcoming from *Inlandia, Sentinel Quarterly Review, Arc-24, Interviewing the Caribbean (IC), Cha, Monkeystarpress, Elsewherelitmag*.


**silent lotus** is a spiritual advisor. His poetry has been published in Europe, England, America, Canada and Australia. Having resided for a significant portion of his life in the Caribbean and The Netherlands he has retained his affiliation with the unique community of Roosevelt, NJ where he was raised. For a number of years he facilitated poetry circles at the Institute For The Study & Practice of Nonviolence in Providence, RI. He lives with the artist Nermin Kura.


**Susan Beth Furst** is a storyteller, poet and haiku artist. She has been published on The Poetry Super Highway, Haiku Universe, The Weekly Avocet, and the upcoming Spring Edition of The Avocet: A Journal of Nature Poetry. She is currently publishing her first fairy tale, *Humpty Dumpty, Cracks and All: A Tale of Hope and Redemption*. You can find her website at beautifuldefect.com. She lives happily in Woodbridge, Virginia with her husband and a canary named Mozart.

**Tammi Truax** works as a teacher and a writer. In 2013 she was editor of *Longfellow's Lady Wentworth; A Poet's Tale* (illustrated) (Bookbaby, 2013), and released her debut novel *Broken Buckets*, as an eBook. Her poems are in several anthologies, most recently *The Widows' Handbook: Poetic Reflections on Grief and Survival*, with a forward by Justice Ginsburg (Kent State University Press, 2014). In 2014 she was the first winner of The Provenance Prize for her story *Daz Herz* and in 2015 she had a short story included in an anthology called *Compass Points* (Piscataqua Press). She blogs at **www.aintiawriter.blogspot.com**.

## Photographs

Grayscale photographs by Jan & Kevin Keough

**F**rontispiece
    'Bowl of Origami micro-chapbooks'

**D**edication
    Mini-schnauzer 'Pixie' with micro-chapbook

**L**earning Kindness
    Angel Trumpet plant, Pacific Palisades, CA

**A**ppreciation
    'Three Dogs at the Door,' Cumberland, RI

**I**ntrospection
    Lake Tomahawk, Black Mountain, NC

**D**ilemma
    Monastery Path, Cumberland, RI

**I**n Praise of Kindness
    Eau Gallie Causeway, Indialantic, FL

**C**hallenge
    Butterfly Garden, Chase Farm, Lincoln, RI

**A**bout The Origami Poems Project
    Clothesline of chapbooks, Wickford Art Gallery

**E**ndpage
    Mini-schnauzer 'Wendy' with micro-chapbooks

# COVER ART

"Rainy Cherry Blossoms" by Lauri Burke

Lauri Burke grew up on the shores of Lake Michigan. She worked the better part of 40 years at the Barrington Public Library in Barrington, RI, where she had the great pleasure of continuing her education in the arts and humanities through her work designing and implementing cultural programming.

Recently retired, Lauri looks forward to diving into the manifold joys of creativity with time to spare. Lauri is happily married to Jeff Burke, and is the proud mother of Flannery Burke.

She has published poetry in a variety of magazines, as well as in the Origami Poems Project.

Lauri has generously created many chapbook covers for the Origami Poems Project. Her work is whimsical and daring – she's a high wire artist of the iPad. We are happy that she enjoys sharing her creations with us!

Visit Lauri Burke's Origami Artist's page to see more of her cover art.  Go to 'Pick an Artist' under the Poets tab on the Home page: www.origamipoems.com.

# About The Origami Poems Project

Since 2009, The Origami Poems Project has been publishing 'free' micro-chapbooks. The poems are cleverly arranged on a single-page PDF that is folded, origami-style, into a palm-sized book. These PDFs are available for download at: www.origamipoems.com

Visit our website to read the work of countless poets. And be sure to print your favorite ones to share at a local coffee shop, library or bookstore. There is a slide show under the 'Who We Are' menu to help you learn to fold.

If you wish, sign up for our occasional newsletter (emailed every 3-4 months). We won't send frequent emails – we haven't the time!

Any questions? Email us: origamipoems@gmail.com

All profits from the sale of this book go to the Origami Poems Project, a 501(c)3 Non-Profit organization.

Thank you.

Jan Keough & Kevin Keough, Editors

## Addendum: Quotes on Kindness

'Remember there's no such thing as a small act of kindness. Every act creates a ripple with no logical end.'
- Scott Adams

'You cannot do a kindness too soon, for you never know how soon will be too late.'
- Ralph Waldo Emerson

'This is my simple religion. There is no need for temples; no need for complicated philosophy. Our own brain, our own heart is our temple; the philosophy is kindness.'
- Dalai Llama

'That best portion of a man's life, his little, nameless, unremembered act of kindness and love.'
- William Wordsworth

'Here are the values that I stand for: honesty, equality, kindness, compassion, treating people the way you want to be treated and helping those in need.'
- Ellen DeGeneres

'Forget injuries, never forget kindness.'
- Confucius

'Wherever there is a human being there is an opportunity for a kindness.' - Seneca

'When we practice loving kindness and compassion, we are the first ones to profit.'
- Rumi

# INDEX OF POETS

## A

Ann Kestner
    Bio, 73
    Language Like Medicine, 46

## B

Bill Carpenter
    Arms Wide Open, 30
    Bio, 73
Bryanna Licciardi
    Bio, 73
    Taking It Back, 6

## C

Carol Aronoff
    Bio, 75
    Make Offerings, 56
Carol Ayer
    All I Have, 8
    Bio, 75
Caroline Johnson
    Bio, 75
    Shut-Ins, 4
Charlene Neely
    Bio, 77
    The Poem I Should Have Written, 34
Chris Toto Zaremba
    Bio, 77
    Left You In The Dark, 29
Christina Sng
    Bio, 77
    When She Cried, 51
Cynthia Anderson
    Angel of Kindness, 64
    Bio, 77

# D

D.G. Geis
  Bio, 79
  Two Kinds, 36
David Allen Sullivan
  Bio, 79
  What Do You Say?, 70

# E

Elizabeth S. Wolf
  Bio, 79
  What If, 43

# F

Frank Beltrano
  Bio, 81
  Dogs and Cats and Places, 23

# G

George Such
  Bio, 81
  Is It Natural To Be Kind,, 45
Gretchen Primack
  Bio, 83
  Holstein, 66

# H

Helen Burke
  Bio, 83
  New Childhood, 68
Helen M. D'Ordine
  Bedtime, 44
  Bio, 83

# J

Jackie Chou

    Bio, 85
    The Difference Kindness Makes, 17
James Penha
    Bio, 85
    Lesson, 18
Jan Chronister
    Bio, 85
    Saint of the Day, 53
Jeffrey Johannes
    Bio, 87
    Faith In Us, 3
Joan Leotta
    Bio, 87
    Hearts, 38
Joely Johnson Mork
    Bio, 87
    Errand, 24

# M

M.j. Iuppa
    Bio, 93
    Kindness-, 55
Marguerite Keil Flanders
    Bio, 87
    February, 22
Marilyn Zelke-Windau
    Bio, 89
    Content, 20
Martin Willitts Jr.
    Bio, 89
    Every Moment Passes And Every Moment Stays Still, 13
Mary C. Rowin
    Bio, 91
    Morning Gift, 47
Mary McCarthy
    Bio, 91
    Years Later, 33
Maryann Russo
    Bio, 89
    The River, 12
Marybeth Rua-Larsen

Bio, 91
The Possum, 69

## P

Padma Prasad
   Bio, 93
   The Ice, 35
Peter Bergquist
   Bio, 93
   Kindness, 21

## R

Ronnie Hess
   Bio, 95
   Ode To An Eleven Year Old Boy, 63
Roz Levine
   Bio, 95
   Her Act of Loving Kindness, 54

## S

Sandra Anfang
   Bio, 95
   Camellias, 10
Shittu Fowora
   Bio, 97
   Whatchamacallit, 58
silent lotus
   Bio, 97
   Rosewood & Inlays, 32
Susan Beth Furst
   Bio, 97
   The Untouchable, 52

## T

Tammi Truax
   Bio, 99
   Duplexity, 5

Wendy
•

# THE ORIGAMI POEMS PROJECT
Helping the world, one, *free* micro-chapbook at a time.

www.ingramcontent.com/pod-product-compliance
Lightning Source LLC
Chambersburg PA
CBHW071512040426
42444CB00008B/1614